May You Shine

LOVE LETTERS to the HURTING, HEALING, and GROWING HEART

May You

Shine

LOVE LETTERS to the HURTING, HEALING, and GROWING HEART

♥ tess hayes

May You Shine: Love Letters to the Hurting, Healing, and Growing Heart
© 2021 Tess Hayes.

Stock Art by: iStock & Vecteezy

ISBN: 978-1-7360257-1-0
Printed in the United States of America
First Printing: 2021
25 24 23 22 21   5 4 3 2 1

To order, visit www.tesshayes.com.

We are all blossoming out of pain and into beauty.
However, even amidst our aching, we are treasures,
and we must never forget that we are all precious
gems, whether we are struggling or succeeding.

May this book remind you of just how special you are,
how wildly capable you are of letting your light shine.

Introduction

I wrote this book to make readers feel like they have a friend sitting right next to them, listening to them and remaining alongside them, for whatever their journey. For it to make people feel like someone is holding their hand and smiling at them, reassuring them that it will be OK. For it to provide warmth and comfort to hurting hearts.

I hope for this book to heal people's wounds and inspire them to stand strong in the face of hardships or discomfort. For it to make people breathe a sigh of relief knowing that they are not alone, that someone understands and sees them. For people to read it and have their soul be at ease.

I hope for these words to foster kindness, love, and connection and inspire people to spread this in the world. For people to feel like they're being hugged tightly by someone who cares about them.

May You Shine addresses the reader exactly as I see them—a beautiful light that only needs love and permission to spread its warmth in the world. This book meets readers in their pain, in their hurt, and carries them through so they can truly grow into the incredibly stunning, unique creations they were meant to be.

Sometimes people just need permission to rest. To cry. To be tired. To fall apart. To make mistakes. They don't need advice or judgment or opinions. All they need is someone to shower them in comfort and grace. Someone to show them what it truly means to be loved.

It is my sincere wish that this book will give you, the reader, that love and support, and that through exploring your own inner being and understanding your own worth, you will learn to shine brightly in this world.

With deepest love,
Tess Hayes

love
letter

I'm sorry for all the times your voice has been silenced.

I'm sorry for all the times you have been **forced to change** in order to **fit in**.

I'm sorry for all the times you have been **walked on** and **away from**.

I'm sorry for all the times your worth and abilities have been **questioned** or **doubted**.

I'm sorry for all the times you have been **misunderstood** and **misrepresented**.

I **see** you. I **hear** you.
I am **with** you.

love
letter 2

You belong.

All of you— **every single inch of you**—has a seat at the table. Not just the prettied-up, smiling, polite version. Not just the successful, well-spoken, put-together version.

No, *all* of you deserves to
shine in this life. This includes
all those parts of yourself
that you try to hide.

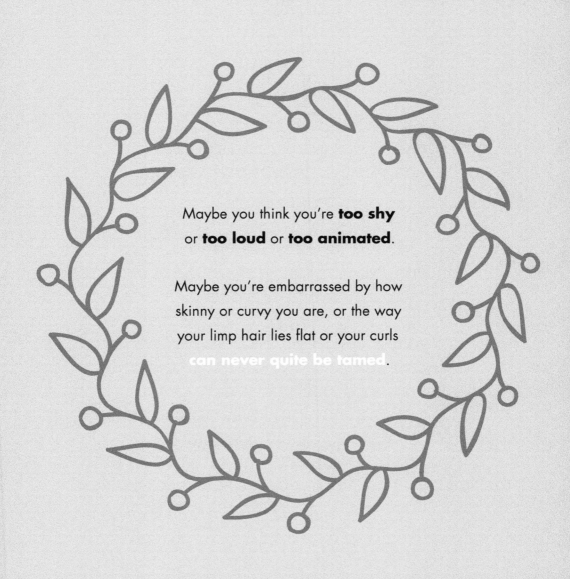

Maybe you think you're **too shy** or **too loud** or **too animated**.

Maybe you're embarrassed by how skinny or curvy you are, or the way your limp hair lies flat or your curls can never quite be tamed.

Maybe, every time you walk into a room,
you wish you were a little less **awkward**.
A little more "normal."

Maybe parts of you are **scared**
and **unsure**, and you do everything you
can to conceal them from others.

We all have some part of ourselves that we
try to change or hide from the world in order to
feel accepted. But the truth is, sweet friend, those
deepest parts of you have **more to offer
than you could ever know**.

If you find the confidence within to simply honor who you are in this very moment—**the courage to let yourself shine**—you'll have a whole new experience of what it means to belong.

You will realize that you have **belonged all along**; you only needed to believe it.

love
letter 3

There will come a day when the pain you thought you couldn't make it through seems to live in the distant past. When the deep worries that kept you up at night are but a passing memory. When the fear and stress that once pulsated throughout your body are **unrecognizable to you**.

It never seems like it at the time, though.
No, it never does. At the time, it seems
like our pain will last forever.

But I'm here to tell you that **this too shall pass.**

If you feel too weak to believe me right now, **that's OK**. Through these pages, I'll hold your hand and walk alongside you until you're strong enough to **see it for yourself**.

love
letter 4

Pain thrives on loneliness; it feeds off isolation. But its greatest enemy is **connection**. No matter how deeply pain has burrowed within your heart, it cannot persevere when faced with a healthy dose of **comfort and community**.

You might hurt, but know that **you don't have to hurt alone**. Our sorrows are always easier to bear when we allow others to walk alongside us on our journey.

Don't close yourself off from the **healing power of community**.

love
letter 5

The little moments,
they come and go.
If you're not careful,
they will slip right by.

You'll miss **the sunset perfectly painting the sky**, the stranger who waits just a little longer to hold the door open for you, the cashier who chooses genuine friendliness over a robotic script, the birds chirping in unison as you walk down the street, the partner who puts their phone down to **be fully present** as you tell them about your day.

Stop waiting.

Stop living in the future.

Stop closing your eyes to the here and now.

And let yourself become fully immersed in the
awe-inspiring moments the universe is
orchestrating all around you.

love
letter 6

Sometimes, you simply want to be held—
not just physically, but emotionally.

You want to know that your heart
is **protected and cared for**.

That, no matter what, you will not be allowed
to fall so far that you can't get back up.

That you have a **community of angels**
who won't let you go through life alone.

This community could be a gathering of people there to support you: family, neighbors, church, friends. Or it could be one person who promises to see you, to hear you, to hold you up even when the winds try to knock you over.

Find your people.

Find your person.

Find your angels.

love
letter 1

Forgiveness is crucial. Forgiveness is what will set us free. But we can't skip straight to this step, for the journey to forgiveness is just as important.

This journey is filled with **communication** and **grace** and **honesty**.

It's filled with acknowledging what happened and choosing to **free yourself** from the shackles of anger rather than live with bitterness and regret the rest of your life.

It's filled with **taking back control** of how your heart feels rather than allowing another person to have this responsibility.

It's filled with **patience** and the understanding that the road may be long and twisted, and you may need to stop often and rest.

It's filled with realizing you may need to build new boundaries in your life in order to move forward.

And it's filled with knowing that you can forgive without agreeing with their words or actions. You can forgive because you have made peace your main priority.

love
letter 8

At times, it can be difficult to realize your own beauty. But, regardless, you are still **stunning, dazzling, amazingly beautiful**.

Every time you pick out your flaws and imperfections—every time you look at another person's body or life or personality and beat yourself up for not having what they have— you are silently hammering away at your heart. You are bullying yourself when all you truly yearn for is to be **loved**.

Try admiring yourself with a fresh pair of eyes.

Eyes that see **resilience** and **strength**.

Eyes that see the exquisiteness and radiance that has always been there.

For when you start to embrace your **beauty** in all its grandeur and show yourself **the respect you deserve**, you in turn invite other people to do the same.

love
letter 9

Sometimes, learning to smile and laugh through the hard days can be what keeps us sane. It can keep us focused on the positive and able to find goodness amid the chaos.

But sometimes, learning to cry and collapse is **just as beautiful**.

Learning that without fully honoring the heavy emotions within us, we can't fully experience the joy within us.

Learning that it's **OK** to **not be OK**.

love
letter 10

You were made on purpose.

You were made with intention.

You were made to shine.

love
letter II

We tend to think that people want
our lives **all put together** and
tied with **a pretty bow** before
we present it to them.

That people want the edited, PG
version of our lives, only focusing
on the joyous highlights.

That people want us to leave out the
dark, messy, not-so-pretty parts.

That this will draw people in and
make them like us more.

And who can blame us? After all,
this is **the easier route to take**.

But what this really does is create distance.
It creates inauthenticity. It creates a world
where people feel more alone and less
connected, where the honest stories of
their lives remain captive inside of them.

It creates a fear of being **different**.

Of being **judged**.

Of being **real**.

Vulnerability is the bridge to connection.
It is **the pathway to truly living**.

Own your story with a badge of honor

and free it to breathe in the open. You never
know who is using it as their inspiration and
survival guide, who is sighing a breath of relief
knowing that they are not alone.

love
letter 12

When you are hurting, when you are tired, when you feel lost in this life—**give yourself permission to pause**.

You do not need to tend to all your plans and to-dos. You do not need to follow a detailed road map showing exactly how to achieve all your goals and dreams. It's OK to just *be* and to trust that the universe is working on your behalf.

Today you're aching, but that doesn't mean that tomorrow you won't be **blooming**. Your present state does not dictate your future state.

So allow yourself to rest, sweet child, clinging to the hope of a **renewed, healed spirit** in due time.

Give your heart what it needs to **tend to itself**.

love
letter 13

You wish you could take it back. You replay the situation **over** and **over** again in your head, each time allowing the regret to sink in just a little **deeper**.

We've all been there.

We've all felt the remorse and shame of our words or actions. Sometimes, the shame is fairly easy to release; other times, it lingers in our bodies, seemingly forever. It affects our mental, physical, emotional, and spiritual selves.

But you **cannot change the past**.

What you can change is how you handle every situation from this moment forward.

Bathe yourself in **self-compassion**. Shower yourself in grace. Give yourself space to feel— truly *feel*. Remind yourself that you are not alone in this journey, that **you have never messed up too badly to begin anew**.

Each moment, you are given the opportunity to choose again. What will you choose?

love
letter 14

Before you feel properly equipped to chase whatever is calling your name, you will feel **unsure** and **inadequate**.

Before you see all the pieces of your life beautifully stitched together and making perfect sense, you will see the broken parts of your life **scattered all over**, nothing quite fitting together or working out the way you'd hoped.

Before you're filled with ease and
contentment, grateful for where you are,
you will be filled with **confusion** and
unanswered questions, waiting
for the right opportunities to arise and
people to come into your life.

Be **patient**. Know that it is common to go through droughts of difficulty before catapulting into the arena of **greatness**.

Hardships do not disqualify you from conquering your life.

love
letter 15

Let the tears flow.

Let the sadness stream out.

It will all be OK, sweet friend. It will all be OK. Maybe not right now, maybe not tomorrow. But you will get through this.

love
letter 16

Be good.

Be polite.

Be happy.

Be quiet.

Be the person who everyone **likes**.

Who doesn't make a **scene**.

Who does what they're **told**.

We've spent so many years being told who to be, but I'm here to tell you to **throw all of that out the window**. Squash any idea of who you think you should be—who you've been conditioned to be.

Instead, just be **you**.

Fully, completely, wildly YOU.

Be a person who listens to their
innermost voice over the voice of others.

Be a person who finds freedom in being their
untamed, authentic self.

If you constantly conform into who others
believe you should be, your true soul will
slowly wither away. But it will bloom beautifully
to life as you unleash the **true you** for all the
world to marvel at and revel in.

love
letter 17

The disease to please is a slow and painful death. It allows every single person *except you* to dictate who you are, how you act, and what you do. It morphs you into someone you don't even know and eats away at your insides until weakness takes over your whole body.

There is a cure for this, though—one that guarantees a **full recovery**. A cure so remarkable that people will begin to look at you in awe of how you are radiating such **vitality** and **joy** and **confidence**.

Self-love.

This miraculous medicine will heal
you **from the inside out**.

It will wipe the layers of fog from your
eyes and allow you to see the world
with renewed and brightened sight.

It will restore your authentic spirit and
ensure you make decisions not out of
a need for approval, but rather out of
a deeply engrained love for yourself.

love
letter 18

Figuring out one's **purpose** is something that people have been trying to chase for centuries and something that continues to linger throughout their entire lives. It always seems like this lofty goal that's never quite attainable, right in front of us and yet **just out of reach**.

Challenge yourself to stop trying so desperately to figure out your purpose. Instead, just **live**.

Share your talents with others, find a new hobby, spread **kindness** to anyone and everyone, embark on an adventure in your backyard or across the world, give to those in need. Laugh.

Getting stuck in your need to have every question answered and your whole life figured out can block the natural flow of **energy** in your life. It inhibits the universe from doing its thing. It clouds your heart and your mind and keeps you from **shining**. It takes you further away from your purpose.

So inhale a deep breath.

Let it out.

Smile.

And go with the flow.

Trust that what is for you will not pass you, and that you are **fulfilling your purpose** each moment you show up as authentically you.

love
letter 19

You can and will never be absolutely
certain where you are going.

You cannot be sure that the path you are
on leads to the **destination you desire**.

You cannot be sure that there isn't a
better opportunity or option out there.

That's the thing about faith.

Having faith requires blind trust that
you are *exactly* where you need to be
at the exact right moment.

Having faith allows you to feel at ease with
what you're doing, who you are, and where
you are on your journey, knowing that you
are neither one step behind nor one step
ahead of **where you should be**.

Try faith on.

Try letting your questioning, uncertain mind **rest**, and allow the quiet, steadfast **conviction of your own soul** to be the only beat you dance to.

Try letting your doubts and fears **dissolve** in the background as your faith paints the foreground of your life with peaceful confidence.

love
letter 20

As much as you might convince yourself of society's lies, let this be a **gentle reminder** that no one has everything together the way they portray themselves.

Everyone has an inner battle they'd rather
put a pretty bow on than expose to the world:

relationships they desperately wish they could mend

habits they struggle to break

addictions that lie hidden behind closed doors

dreams that have been trampled

past traumas still eating away at their soul.

The next time you wonder why you can't
seem to get this whole *life* thing figured out,
remember that **you are not alone**.

Be patient with yourself and know that you
are **simply taking it one step at a time**,
along with everyone else. Don't fool yourself
into believing there is anything wrong with you
for experiencing these valleys of life. This only
makes you human—just like everybody else.

love
letter 21

CELEBRATE.

Celebrate the **momentous**
and the **seemingly ordinary**.

Celebrate the patiently awaited
promotion at work.

Waking up thirty minutes
earlier than yesterday

Giving **birth** to a healthy baby.

Saying **no** to that brownie.

Passing the **test** you've been
studying so diligently for.

Remaining **calm** when your
spouse pokes that button of yours.

It's so easy to be hyperaware of the annoying or difficult parts of your day. It's even easier to gloss right over the incredible things happening all around you.

But there is **always** a reason to celebrate—if you only look for it.

love
letter 22

Healing is not linear.

It is a complicated choreography, a
seemingly random sequence of one step
forward, followed by two steps backward.

It is feeling **hopeful** about the **future**, followed by feeling **stagnant** in your **growth**.

It is learning from your **mistakes**, followed by making **the same mistakes again**.

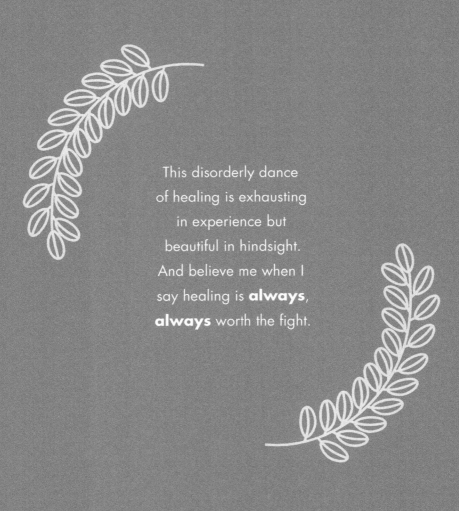

This disorderly dance
of healing is exhausting
in experience but
beautiful in hindsight.
And believe me when I
say healing is **always**,
always worth the fight.

love
letter 23

Sitting in the silence can be **uncomfortable**. It can seem pointless, even boring. But sitting in the silence allows your soul the space it needs to **speak**. It keeps your innermost voice from being drowned out by the day-to-day noise.

Your mind will try to play tricks on you by telling you that you don't need to slow down.

That you can keep **distracting yourself** with more responsibilities and activities.

That the only voices you need to pay attention to are external ones.

That this **hamster wheel of life** you're on will lead you to where you're supposed to be.

But I promise you that your answers will **not**
be found in the chaos, but rather in the stillness.
What you truly need is to give your heart
permission to **communicate and be heard**.

Your heart has magical things to tell you;
you only need to quiet your mind and **listen**.

love
letter 24

Do not fall in love with someone hoping
for them to complete you. No person
should ever be given this responsibility.

Fall in love with someone hoping for
them to **enhance** and **elevate** the
person you already are.

Come to them fully complete, fully **whole**.

Come to them knowing that a **magical force** between two people can only be created when each of you **already possesses** a sense of self-confidence, self-love, and inner peace.

No one else can do your growth and healing for you, so don't expect them to. I **promise** you that doing so will leave you feeling empty every single time.

Instead, learn to connect with yourself. Take the time to listen to the gentle whisperings of your soul, feed it what it's begging for, give it the rest it **requires** and the adventure it **desires**.

Embark on a journey of self-discovery so
that you've filled the emptiness with love and
made **a home within your own heart**.

Then, and only then, will you be able
to experience what it means to fall in love
from a place of **wholeness**.

love
letter 25

They say that change is **hard**.

You know what's even **harder**? Remaining the same.
Getting to the end of your life and realizing every dream,
every goal, every aspiration of yours is **still inside you**.

But bottling up your dreams inside your soul is
cheating the world of your unique magic that can have
a magnificent impact on the lives of so many.

Awaken your spirit, feed that hungry fire within you,
and make whatever changes are necessary to align the
reality of who you are with your vision of who you want
to be so that you can grow into your beautiful self.

love
letter 26

Let this serve as a reminder that your struggles do not make you "less than" or hopeless. Your struggles make you **human**. They mean you are enduring one of the demons that every soul encounters at some point along their walk.

It's **OK** that you are **not OK**.

Please **do not give up on yourself**. This dark valley of your life was never meant to fully consume who you are, but simply to act as a stopping point along your journey. You may be at the bottom of the hill, but if you look up long enough, you will see an awe-inspiring, beautiful peak to this mountain as well. The sun is radiating upon it, inviting you to step into its warm and welcoming rays.

So **hurt** and **break** and **collapse** as
you honor the war raging within you.

Then, awaken the **warrior**
within you and stand tall.

Look your demon in the eye and
say, "**Not today**." It may have won
some of the battles, but you refuse to
allow it to win the war.

love
letter 27

You'll find that some people in your life are best loved from afar.

Doing this does not make you a bad person.

love
letter 28

You do not create boundaries to push people away. You create them to tell your own soul, "I respect you. I will take care of you."

love
letter 29

A compassionate heart is one that has
known hurt but **extends love nonetheless**.

It has felt betrayal but responds with grace.

It chooses to see an avenue for connection
amidst a million reasons to withdraw.

A compassionate heart has a world-healing
combination of both **strength** and **gentleness**,
and it should be treated with the utmost care.

Especially by its owner.

Especially by **you**.

love
letter 30

When the anger or frustration or sadness sets in, **let it in**. Open your doors to it; don't push it away. Doing so only forces you to face it later, and by that point, it will have bubbled over into a multiplied version of what it originally was.

We always think that it's unhealthy to be upset or feel down, but that's like telling someone it's wrong to be **human**.

The only thing that's unhealthy about our emotions is when we allow them to take over us.

Feel your feelings and feel them **deeply**.

Then, let them move through you
and out of you. Set them free.

This is the beautiful
cycle of life.

love
letter 31

You can do more than you give yourself credit for.

You know that thing you get so nervous thinking about you want to throw up? That thing you've convinced yourself you're incapable of for so long?

You can do it. But you must give yourself the opportunity to prove your doubts wrong.

Immerse yourself in situations that will allow you to **amaze** yourself.

Allow yourself to embrace your fears in order to see that they can't stop you from **flourishing**.

love
letter 32

Some days, you will rely on others to carry you through the darkness enveloping your life. When you're too weak to stand on your own, you will turn to them to **pick you up**, provide you with light and direction, and help **guide you home**.

And then there will be days when others come to **you** for strength and encouragement. They will look to you to **hold them** in their hardship and walk alongside them on their journey. They will need you to **shine** for them.

We were never meant to completely depend on other people, nor were we made to always be the rock for others.

Life is a constant flow of give-and-take. Being in balance with this rhythmic tide helps us realize that we are all connected and doing what we can to walk each other home.

love
letter 33

When they hurt you, know that it is
because **they, too, are hurting**.

Their actions and words may appear to be filled with
disrespect or malice, but those are just the outward
projections they've allowed you to see. When you look
beyond them, you will find a soul simply wanting to be
loved, wanting to be seen, wanting to belong.

Choose to be the person that does this for them.
Choose to be gentle. Choose to be patient. Choose to
be **forgiving**. Choose to be **compassionate**.

Choose to **listen**, not with your ears, but with your **heart**.

love
letter 34

There will be times in your life that require you to **make a decision**, times that require you to ask yourself if the life you're living now is the life you want to live in ten years. If the answer is no, then I hope and pray you find the strength within you to determine what habits or actions or thoughts you need to transform to lead you to **the future you want**.

You are the only person with the ability
to **mold your life** into a creation you
admire with pride and amazement.

You are not one moment too late to begin
working on this **masterpiece** either. One
of the most precious gifts you have been
given is that whether you're twenty or fifty
or eighty years old, you still have the ability
to wake up and say, "I'm going to do this
differently. I'm going to make a change."

So, shift.

Shift your life, **day** after **day** after **day**,
as many times as your soul requests. Do it
with confidence and excitement, and watch
as your beautiful life unfolds before you.

love
letter 35

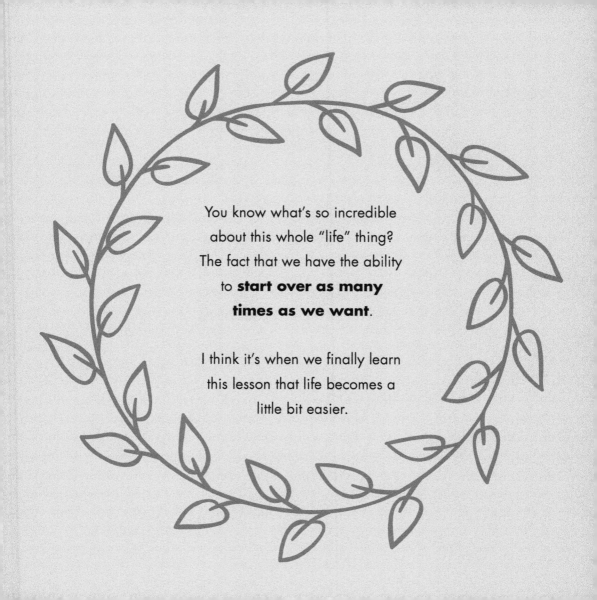

You know what's so incredible
about this whole "life" thing?
The fact that we have the ability
to **start over as many
times as we want**.

I think it's when we finally learn
this lesson that life becomes a
little bit easier.

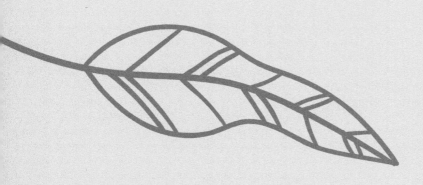

You can fall, and you can take steps
backwards. And then you can **get back up**;
you can rebuild yourself. Today, and tomorrow,
and the next day, and the next.

You are not perfect. Life is messy. And yet you
can always decide that *this* is the moment you
will choose again. You will choose differently.
You will start fresh.

The fact is, you will never reach a certain destination and be fully, 100 percent the person you want to become. Because you are human, and you will screw up, and you will struggle.

But you can also wipe yourself off and stand back up. **Every single day**. You hold this resilience within you. And that, my friend, is where your power lies.

love
letter 36

Relationships are life's greatest teachers. They present to us what is still unhealed inside of ourselves. They show us which aspects of our hearts **still need work**.

So, when someone's actions make you feel **triggered**—make you fall into old thought patterns or response mechanisms—peel back the layers and assess what part of you still needs tending to. Be thankful that you've been given this **chance** to work on mending the hurting pieces of your soul.

Every single relationship, whether wonderful or terrible, provides us with an incredible opportunity to learn what life is trying to teach us.

If we fail to learn from our relationships, life will continue to present us with the same lesson over and over until we have finally mastered it.

love
letter 37

Do not rely on anyone else to carry you toward
your dreams or fight for them the way that you can.

Yes, you should **ask for help** when you need it,
and that will probably be often. You should seek
out advice and knowledge from those who have
experience. You should foster relationships with
people who **truly want to help you shine**.

But ultimately, *you* must be your biggest advocate. You
must listen to your own heart when making decisions,
put in the strenuous work, *be your own hype man*.

For the whisperings of your heart speak more
strongly to you than to anyone else, and it is *you*
who can best fulfill your heart's desires.

love letter 38

Your heart knows better than any textbook, professional, panelist, or podcast. Your gut has an **innate instinct** that should never be undermined.

So, when someone tells you something with confidence and conviction, but a nagging inside of you is **telling you differently**, always listen to your gut. Always follow the guidebook and advice of your own spirit, your own soul.

love
letter 39

You were made **with** purpose,
on purpose, and **for** a purpose.
And that specific purpose is ever evolving,
ever changing. Just like your friends, career,
body, hobbies, and mind, your purpose
is constantly being shaped and molded to
adapt to the present you.

But it is crucial to keep in mind that if you make your purpose all about you, you will search for it your entire life. It is not about you, but rather about how you can **utilize** your unique gifts and talents to serve others. It is about how you will **transform the world** rather than be transformed.

This mindset of **selflessness** and **generosity** and **compassion** will open doors that weren't there before and create ease where difficulty and confusion once reigned.

It is through giving of ourselves that we, in turn, find ourselves.

love
letter 40

True love is not easy, but it's worth it.

It's not free from mistakes but filled with forgiveness.

It's not constant laughs and smiles but
an abundance of **grace** and **comfort**.

You see, true love is not perfect. It's two flawed souls
coming together as one to help each other heal, grow, and
thrive. It's accepting the other's past, present, and future
and saying: "I want it all—the beautiful and the hard parts."

Don't find yourself a partner that strives to be perfect or
only loves you at your best. Rather, find yourself a partner
that strives to be **honest**, **devoted**, and **zealous** in the
pursuit of loving every single crevice of your soul.

love
letter 41

It happened, and you
cannot change it.

It's OK.

Sit with your feelings.
Feel your feelings.

Inhale. Exhale. Cry.
Slow down and just be.

Repeat.

You will get through this.

love
letter 42

Judging is the **easy** thing to do.
It has become our way of protecting
ourselves, of defending our thoughts
and values and accepted ways of life.
It has become our **comfort zone**.

But this world has enough criticism
and enough disunity.

Do not allow the differences between yourself and another to form a divisive barrier between you. Decide to see the person or situation you don't agree with (or maybe just don't understand) with eyes of **curiosity** instead.

While everyone else is quick to judgment,
be the person who is quick to compassion,
quick to grace, quick to understanding.
Doing so does not necessarily say that
you are in alignment with another's
choices, but it does say that you
choose to put love above all else.

All ways.

Always.

love
letter 43

You may have been
turned down and looked over
more times than you can **count**.

You may have watched
as **person** after **person**
pushed you to the ground.

You may have felt the sting of
rejection or **disapproval** more
deeply than you knew was possible.

It may have been a boss

a spouse

a friend

a child

a boyfriend

a girlfriend

a parent.

Regardless of who caused these bruises in your life, you can put the power back in **your own hands**. You can wear your scars as **badges of honor**, as reminders that your daily strength and perseverance are your most beautiful qualities.

You own your life.

You own your choices.

You own your heart.

Don't let anyone take that ownership away from you.

love
letter 44

You have a **powerful story to share**.
Do not rob the world of your unique message.
Do not silence your voice because your fear
stands taller and speaks louder than the truth of
your convictions within.

People may laugh at you or ignore you or
judge you. And that's OK, because your words
were never meant to connect with everyone.

But they were meant to connect with *someone*.

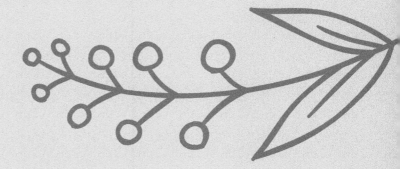

Even if just **one single person** sitting out there in the world feels less alone, less afraid, less alienated because you had the courage to stand up and share your story, doesn't that make it worth doing?

Sometimes sharing your heart
with the world is scary.

Sometimes it seems insignificant.

Sometimes it seems overwhelming.

And sometimes we convince ourselves that
we have nothing of worth to say.

But never downplay
how much sharing your
authentic self with the
world can truly impact the
lives of others—whether
that's thousands, hundreds,
or even just one.

love
letter 45

You know you're making progress
when you start to feel **uncomfortable**.

When you make decisions not
out of habit but out of intention.

When you introduce different environments
and voices and goals into your life.

When every molecule in your body wants to run
back toward the **familiar**, but you force yourself to
press on toward the **unknown** instead.

It's in these moments where we shed old layers of what
we've simply become accustomed to and begin to evolve into
who we were **always destined to be**.

love
letter 46

I pray that you never give up on yourself. I pray that you fight hardest for yourself. I pray you always speak kindly to yourself.

I pray that you hold your own hand when no one else can. That you infuse your mind with words of truth. That you learn how to hug yourself tightly, even when your soul feels weary.

I pray that you learn to view yourself as the stunning creation you are and never doubt your innate worth.

I pray that you fall madly, wholly, and deeply in love with yourself. And that you continue doing so every day for the rest of your life.

love
letter 47

Faith is a funny thing.

When your life is in alignment, faith seems
easy, effortless, natural. But when hardship
comes knocking on your door, faith can
suddenly seem **an impossible feat**.

It's as if you forget about all the goodness that's
happened to you. You forget about the times
you were tired and weak and yet you managed
to find the strength within to keep going.

You forget about the times you collapsed
to your knees, **begging** God to save you,
and sure enough, His mighty, healing hands
lifted you out of your suffering.

You forget about the times when you felt
your world **crumbling** around you and yet
you rose, and the pieces of the rubble slowly
reformed into beautiful new beginnings.

We practice **maintaining** our faith during
the good times so that faith is our natural
response in the hard times.

Have faith.

When you encounter those difficult periods,
look back and know that you have made it
through everything—**absolutely everything**—
up until this point. And you will continue to find
the strength to keep going.

love
letter 48

Difficult emotions have a way of
seeping into your heart without
asking for permission. It's like they think
they can come and go as they please.

And as a good host, you should allow
them to always feel welcome, to know
they always have a place to stay.

But remind them that it's a **temporary visit**, and they will not be allowed to make decisions or take control. They will not offer counsel or advice or tell you what to do. They will be graciously given a safe place for as long as they need, but then they must be on their way. Your heart can be their shelter for the time being, but not their permanent home.

You see, the more you try to push your difficult emotions away, the more they will **keep knocking at the door**, until you have no choice but to face them.

Instead of putting so much effort into avoiding them, try **honoring them** without allowing them to consume you. The temporary pain you feel from acknowledging them—then showing them the door—will fade into the past as you slip into lasting peace.

love
letter 49

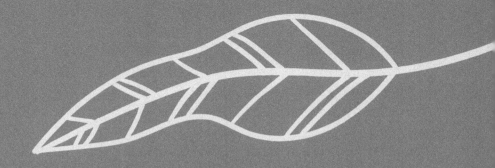

If someone walks away from you, let them.
You should never have to convince someone
to want you. You should never have to beg for
someone to finally see that **you're enough**.

It's easy to believe that doing so will bring them
back and, with them, a sense of being accepted.

A sense of ease and comfort.

A sense of being everything you need to be.

But, sweet friend, this desperate energy you're
putting out only attracts harmful negativity to your life.

Your inability to look within and see that
you have always been more than enough just as you are
leaves your heart vulnerable to being bruised. It is you
telling your soul that you are not willing to give it what
it deserves. That you must rely on an external source
for validation of who you are.

Do not put such a prized treasure as your
own soul in the hands of someone else.

Stand tall in all your **magnificence**
and know that you were never made to
prove yourself to anyone.

Own every single part of who you are,
and walk away from anyone who does
not build you up and anything that does
not remind you of **your innate worth**.

love
letter 50

There is nowhere, no one, and nothing that will provide as many answers as **your own heart**. You can look outward to find meaning and purpose, but you will end up running in circles, and you will tire easily. I promise you that no job, no relationship, no addiction, no external escape can bring you where you need to be.

The answer has always been **within**.

The **road map** to help you on your journey
has always been within.

The **guiding forces** that will lead you where
you need to go have always been within.

Everything you have been searching for is
already available to you.

All the external sources that seem to provide answers are **simply distractions**—do not be misled by them. Instead, allow your soul to do the talking, and you will find yourself exactly where you need to be.

love letter 51

You will **not** be exploding with
excitement and energy every day.

You will **not** feel on fire and aligned
with your passion every day.

You will **not** be overwhelmed with
inspiration and motivation every day.

And guess what? That is perfectly
normal and **OK**.

You don't need to perform a miracle.
You just need to say *yes*.

Yes to consciously finding beauty in all things.
Yes to choosing adventure and pursuing drive
over idleness. But also, yes to recharging, yes
to resting, yes to **simply being**.

Even the sun sets each night before it rises and shines brightly the next morning. And so must you, my darling. In order to really dazzle the world, you must first slow down and fill yourself up with the **nourishment** your soul needs to simply say *yes*.

love
letter 52

When you find yourself **burdened** by life's battles,
unsure of how to make it another step, find solace
in the knowledge that you were made for this. You
were made for *this exact moment*. God has already
weighed each of your battles to ensure it was not
too great for you to face. He breathed strength,
conviction, and hope into you as your armor.

Don't give up mid-fight. You may be tired,
but you are also **victorious**.

Hold firm to God's hand, knowing that you
are being led by someone whose love for you
triumphs over death itself.

love
letter 53

Wherever you go, you plant seeds of your soul. Whether it's what you say to the stranger next to you in line, or how you make others in the room feel, or what you choose to pour your time into, you are constantly **making your mark on the world**.

Your energy is **powerful**; it can be felt by people near and far. Be **intentional** with the way you choose to engage with everything and everyone around you. Your words, actions, expressions, emotions—they all can have a **profound effect** on our society.

Choose to let the **seeds of your soul** create connection, beauty, and joy in a world that so desperately craves it.

love
letter 54

People are hungry to be seen. They **yearn**
to be understood and to belong.

You can offer this to them.

You can **harness** this incredible ability
to bridge the gap, to open the circle,
to reach out your hand.

Too often, we spend our time thinking about our wants, our needs, our hardships. We wait for others to come to us, to ask us how we are, to make us feel included, to assure us that we are OK. That we are enough.

But I beg you to **open your eyes** and **your heart** to see that everyone you meet is in need of this exact same thing.

So, step outside of yourself
and channel your energy toward
others. Strangers, friends, family,
acquaintances—every person you meet
craves to **be seen** and to **be loved.**

Give them this gift. It is your duty;
it is your privilege.

love
letter 55

All too often, we fail before we even start. We downplay our **abilities** and **talents**, convincing ourselves that others can do it better, others have more experience, others have already done it.

But, when your dreams first bloomed inside your heart, they didn't know comparison; they only knew **passion**. Somewhere along the way, your mind's fear became stronger than your soul's beliefs. You quieted the desires of your heart with a steady stream of untruths about who you are, what you are **capable** of, and **why you are here**.

Dig back up the innocence of your dreams.

Unearth the **conviction** and **confidence**
within you that knows no boundaries or envy.

The world needs what your neighbor has to offer, just as it needs exactly what you were created to share. It needs you to **take pride** in your dreams and use them to create a path of blazing light for everyone around you.

love
letter 56

You are a warrior. You are a mother-freaking *warrior*.

You do not sit idly and watch the days
pass you by. No—you pursue each day with
a **tenacity** and **passion** that cannot be tamed.
Your roots are planted deep and have grown
strong, allowing you to hold firm against
anything that tries to take you down.

You are a source of greatness, and your fierce,
magical light **radiates** throughout the whole world.

love
letter
57

Your silence speaks more loudly than you think. It **echoes** into the lives of people begging for help. It **ricochets** in cities desperate for your support. It serves as a **powerful message** to those in need that they are alone in their fight.

So use your voice.

Use your **talents**.

Use your **hands** and your **feet**.

You don't need a platform or status or followers or fame or wealth to pave a path of healing in this world. You just need to do what you **can**, where you **are**, with what you **have**. Your actions will overtake your silence, and this world will be washed anew with hope.

love letter 58

Remember when you were **hurting**, but the
world just kept spinning? When you were stuck
in a place of **heartache**, but everyone else was
moving on with their lives as normal?

It was a **painful**, **lonely** place to be.

Look around and make it your honor to
ensure you stand alongside anyone feeling this way.
Make a promise to yourself that your heart will be open
and arms will be outstretched to all who come into your
life. **No one** should be forgotten about or left to fight
through their hardships on their own. Let them **know**
that, in you, they have someone who will walk with them,
someone who will hold their hand until the storm passes
and the sunshine begins to sparkle again.

love
letter 59

May your heart be at peace knowing that
you are **already more than enough**.

May you smile with ease knowing that this
world craves **exactly** what you have to offer.

May you be filled with comfort knowing that you have
the ability to bring overwhelming love and light to others
simply by being your **genuine**, **beautiful** self.

May you shine.

About the Author

Tess Hayes has a deep desire to bring healing to this world, constantly yearning to make it a gentler, kinder place to live. Writing is her way of merging her passion and talent with serving others—a magical intersection of possibilities. Ever since she was a young girl, Tess has found freedom in letting her soul speak through putting pen to paper, letting the words flow, and expressing her truest emotions. She strives to be a catalyst for connection, love, and compassion, and her heart is fullest whenever she is able to bring a smile to someone's face. She currently resides in Minneapolis, MN, where she was born and raised, and finds joy in spending time with her friends and family, soaking up nature, adventuring, creating, and staying active.